Art to the young child is more than a matter of painting pictures or making objects. It is a means by which he expresses his individuality and communicates his ideas about himself and his world. Addressed to both parents and teachers of young children, this book answers many of the questions adults ask about children's art and provides refreshing insights into the needs and abilities of the pre-school child.

Its fundamental educational approach, based on actual teaching methods used in the classes of the Art Center of The Museum of Modern Art, leads toward understanding and helping the young child in his growth. The features most characteristic of painting, modeling, and construction at each age level—three, four, and five years—are described and explained in terms of children's changing motivations and capabilities. The concluding section suggests suitable tools and materials and guideposts for stimulating natural expression without stifling it with outworn formulas. The book is illustrated with works by children in classes at the Art Center.

art of the young child

art of the young child

understanding and encouraging creative growth in children three to five

Jane Cooper Bland

The Museum of Modern Art, New York

Distributed by New York Graphic Society Ltd., Greenwich, Connecticut

Published by The Museum of Modern Art, 1968
11 West 53 Street, New York, New York 10019
All rights reserved
First edition, 1957
Second edition, 1960
Third edition, revised, 1968
Library of Congress Catalogue Card Number 68–20399
Designed by Donald Edmund Munson
Printed in Denmark

preface

Until quite recently, the early years of children's art development were not considered important by either teachers or parents. The child's efforts were looked upon only as daubs of paint or shapeless masses of clay. It was thought that the young child could acquire nothing of basic art concepts or skills. His teaching, therefore, was left to those who had little or no experience in the arts. As a result of extensive study, this attitude has completely changed and the ages from three to five years are recognized as one of the most vital and fruitful periods in the creative development of the individual.

The Art Center of The Museum of Modern Art has pioneered in exploring new and better methods in the development of children's creative growth. It was one of the first to offer classes for children as young as three. In 1950, the Art Center introduced classes for parents and children working together and this idea has since been adopted in many schools and museums throughout the country. Only teachers of exceptional training and experience with this age level are selected for classes of three- to five-year-olds at the Center.

This book by Jane Cooper Bland is devoted to an understanding of the creative growth of the young child. It is not merely theoretical, but it has a fundamental educational approach based on actual teaching methods used in the classes of The Art Center of The Museum of Modern Art. Mrs. Bland, an outstanding authority on art education, has particular interest in this area, and has made several studies and experiments which have added to the knowledge and enrichment in guiding creative growth of young children.

Victor D'Amico Director
Department of Education and The Art Center of the Institute of Modern Art
The Museum of Modern Art

5

introduction

    This book is addressed to parents and teachers of young children and to all who are interested in their development. It deals with one of the most important aspects of children's growth: creative expression.

    Art to the child is more than a matter of painting pictures or making objects. It is a means by which he expresses his individuality and communicates his ideas about himself and his world. There is no question that children's art is fascinating to those who enjoy spontaneity and design for their own sake. However, it also has particular significance as an insight into the way children express their ideas and feelings. The art of the young child is probably the most difficult for the average adult to understand. It may appear to be mere scribbles and color patches or fantastic shapes made of clay and other materials. Nevertheless, these are extremely important. They have real meaning for the child and can be guideposts toward understanding and helping him in his growth.

Jane Cooper Bland Instructor
The Art Center of the Institute of Modern Art
The Museum of Modern Art

contents

1

how children create 9

2

fundamentals of art education 44

3

how adults can help 48

1

how children create

understanding children's growth

Young children work spontaneously, trying out their ideas and tools. The forms that they make have meaning to them, although often these are unrecognizable to adults. The child at this age does not usually regard what he has made as a painting or piece of sculpture. He lives through a series of experiences as he paints or models and his final creation might be compared to a motion picture of which we see only the last frame. The finished product reveals very little of the variety and richness of experience the child has gained in the process. Often a deep impression made on a child shows up days or weeks later in a painting or in some other medium, and then he may or may not put his feelings about it into words.

Children invent colors, and mixing color becomes a real adventure when they realize that they have made a new color all by themselves. Each child applies paint in his own way. Some children use staccato brush strokes; some tend to make linear paintings; some make great swishing strokes; while others paint patches, either side by side or overlapping, producing different colors where the patches go over each other. Some paint in different ways at different times.

When it comes to using clay, children squeeze and pat it, exploring its particular character. Some children make large compact forms, some arrange tiny clay shapes into a group, some build high towers, while others string their clay in shapes like cars of a train the whole length of the table top.

Children enjoy choosing various materials of different textures, patterns, and colors, and combining them in pasted pictures called collages. When a child experiments with such materials as burlap, bark, or leather and puts them together into a design that satisfies him, he is developing sensitivity to the qualities of materials. Starting with actual materials has a particular value for a child who for one reason or another has become unsure of himself in painting. All of this increases his power to weigh choices, to discriminate, and both to use and understand the things that make up his everyday world.

Growth manifests itself in a variety of ways. When encouraged to work in his own way, a child will grow in independence. Not only will he ask for less help but he will be able to get started more easily and be less distracted. As he works with greater sureness and absorption, his ideas will flow more freely and he will become less and less concerned with standards other than his own.

Another indication of the child's growth is increasing awareness of colors in relation to each other and in the things he sees around him. In the same way, he becomes

9

more sensitive to the wealth of forms and shapes in his environment. In the classes at the Art Center, for example, children of three soon begin to talk about colors. One child will show the teacher her pink dress and another his new red shoes. Children proudly announce, "I've made the color of my new sweater." Parents have often commented that, after their children have begun painting they show greater interest in colors in their homes and in the choice of new colors for walls and furnishings.

Ability to express feelings and ideas with more power through gradual mastery of the materials he is using is also an evidence of growth.

Children do not grow at an even pace and each work is not always a step forward. Sometimes it seems as if they make one step forward and two backward before there is any definite advance. Therefore, if the child has been doing work that appears attractive and finished, but changes to a stage that seems sloppy and unfinished, this should not be regarded as a failure. It may represent a new effort or a more challenging area of

exploration. It is important to think of growth in terms of a fairly long span of time. Allow children to be three before they are four and don't try to push a child into doing what older children do before he is ready to move ahead.

Because no two children are alike, it is impossible to place them arbitrarily in categories. Many children at three will paint like five-year-olds and vice versa. Some children at four will resemble three-year-olds in painting while their clay modeling may be like that of a five-year-old. This does not mean that if a four-year-old exhibits the achievement of a three-year-old he is retarded or that he is superior if he does work in advance of his age level. It merely shows that children's art expressions vary according to their experience, perception, and maturity. While there is no definite behavior pattern for each year by which a child can be labeled as a three- or four-year-old, there are certain characteristics that identify these ages and help us understand their creative needs and interests.

11

the child at three years

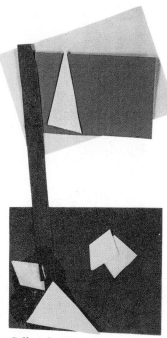

Collage by Mara, 3 years

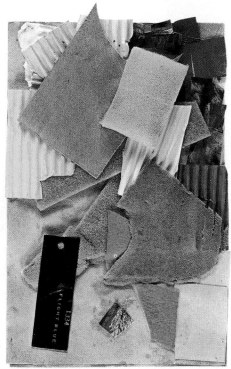

Collage by Randy, 3½ years

Painting by Corinne, 3 years

Painting by Marc, 5 years. Not all children of the same age work and develop in the same way. Marc, who is five years old, paints like a three-year-old.

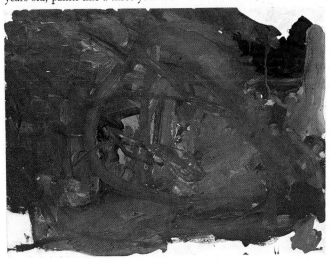

13

Fierce Animal with Many Legs by Kinyon, 3 years.
Kinyon made several paintings of animals after a visit
to the zoo.

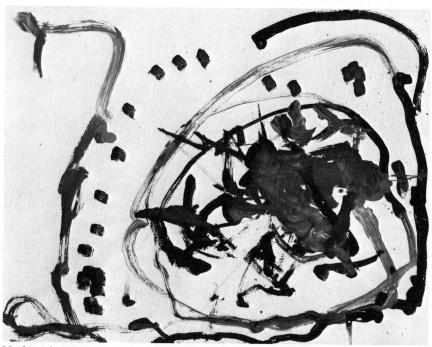

Noah's Ark with All the Animals by Joshua, 3 years

14

the child at three years

In general, three-year-old boys and girls like and need to manipulate materials and to change what they are making as they work. They also take pleasure in doing the same kinds of things over and over. Perhaps they do this in order to convince themselves that they know how or they may just be repeating an enjoyable experience. They often keep changing the colors on their papers by painting one over another until the result is a mass of brown paint. Although this may make the painting less attractive to the adult, the value for the child has been his growing power to change colors. This is an important part of learning.

They pat and roll clay, build it up into some form, squash it, then pat and roll it again; they make birthday cakes, admire them, and pull them apart and start over. A child of three begins constructing by sticking things into clay or any soft material. As a rule, he is not able to cope with mobiles or constructions which require skill in joining, nor can he manage many materials like wire or pipe cleaners.

Most three-year-olds are able to cut paper and they get a great deal of satisfaction from it. They cut paper into pieces for the sheer enjoyment of cutting or because they feel a sense of power in changing the sheet of paper from its original form. Cutting is an activity complete in itself and usually quite separate from pasting. Three-year-olds will cut many small pieces and then push them all aside and choose new materials when they decide to paste. Pasting, too, tends to be a separate activity enjoyed for itself. They often cover what they have made by pasting one piece of paper after another over it. They derive pleasure from manipulating the smooth slippery paste.

Although the child at this age level will occasionally concentrate on any one of the above activities for nearly an hour, most three-year-olds' interest will last only from about five to twenty minutes.

Clay shapes by Mary, 3 years

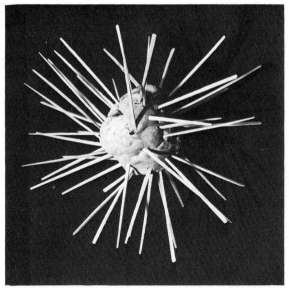

Porcupine by June, 3 years

the child at three years

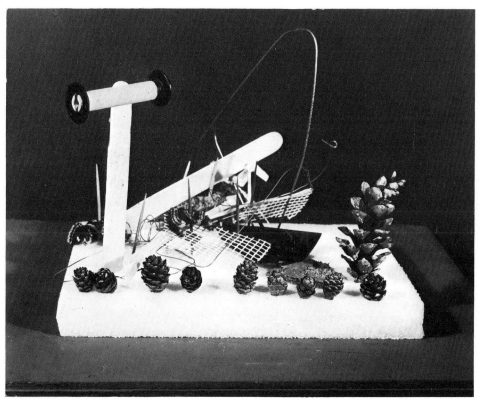

Construction by Carolyn, 3¼ years

the child at three years

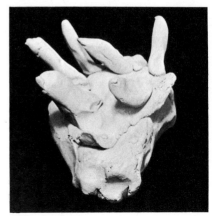

Clay piece by Victor, 3¼ years

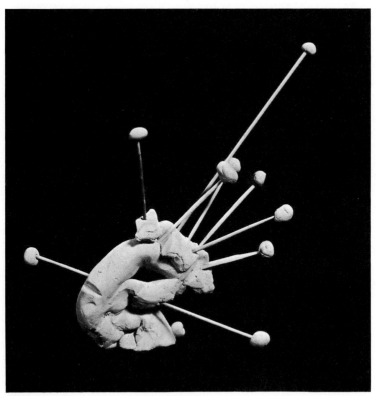

Clay and stick construction by Rita, 3¾ years

the child at four years

For the most part, four-year-olds concentrate longer than three-year-olds. Ten or fifteen minutes to half an hour is an average; some will work for almost an hour. They enjoy both manipulating materials and the power to change what they are making as they work, but they are less inclined to repeat and are not so apt to paint their hands as are the three-year-olds. They make more definite forms, enclosed circular shapes, for example, and they paint masses of color next to each other instead of over one another. A child may elaborate a shape by painting color within it or around it or by surrounding it with other shapes or dots of color. A shape may suggest something representational to him, for instance, a circle as a head, which he may develop by putting features in it. Children at this age tend to use the whole paper, relating linear forms to it and often covering it completely with color. Sometimes they start with a specific idea of what they want to paint while at other times they improvise as they go along.

In clay modeling, most children at four make definite things, building and adding rather than pulling apart and redoing. They are more selective, choosing materials for a collage and placing them with greater deliberation before pasting. They begin to cut and invent instead of only cutting and changing. A four-year-old enjoys making simple constructions and mobiles with wire or pipe cleaners. He needs help with tying or connecting but he can choose and combine materials that can be put together easily.

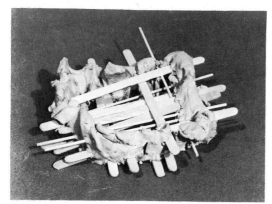

A Trap by Danny, 4 years

Clay construction by Liz, 4½ years

the child at four years

Airport by Peter, 4½ years

the child at four years

Birds' Home by Paula, 4 years. Paula made little birds sitting on nests and a home for them to go into when it rained.

Superman by Brad, 4 years

A Tepee with Two Indians Outside by Nina, 4 years

the child at four years

Collage by Ann, 4 years

Collage by Susan, 4 years

Painting by Paul, 4 years

Painting by Kate, 4 years

the child at five years

As children grow, their span of concentration increases. Therefore, five-year-olds concentrate longer than children of four, sometimes drawing, painting, modeling, or constructing for as long as an hour but usually from about fifteen minutes to half an hour.

They are inclined to preplan their paintings and to make positive shapes, even when making what they call "designs." They mix colors with greater sureness and discrimination than they did in the earlier years. Some, however, still tend to manipulate paint and change their work by painting one color over another repeatedly. This is particularly true of children who are painting for the first time.

In clay modeling, children of this age are apt to combine forms and to build better-constructed objects than those made by either three- or four-year-olds. As they become familiar with the material, they make more complex clay pieces and are apt to select whatever they apply to the clay, such as swab sticks, buttons, straws, to embellish it as a planned part of the construction rather than for the mere satisfaction of sticking things in and taking them out again. Usually they do not repeat for the sake of manipulating the material as a three-year-old will, but tend to create some specific thing. What a child finally produces may develop while he is modeling or from an idea he had at the outset.

A five-year-old chooses materials for collage thoughtfully and cuts them into interesting shapes. He can use scissors with more certainty and skill. He enjoys making constructions and mobiles and can devise ways of fastening materials together with wire, pipe cleaners, paper clips, or yarn, and can begin to balance one shape with another. Like the four-year-old, he learns to look at materials in new ways, particularly as they affect each other. This gives materials a new dimension because the child sees them freshly, as elements that can be converted into original designs through his imagination. He can make constructions that stand by themselves or he can make mobiles, in which the enchantment of motion is an added element.

Alligator by Earl, 5 years

Collage by Laura, 5 years

Painting by Eugene, 5¾ years

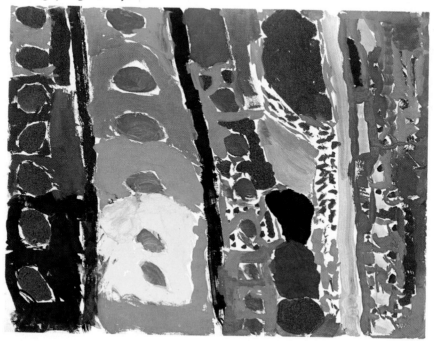

the child at five years

Painting by Patricia, 3¾ years. Not all children of the same age
work and develop in the same way. Patricia, who is three years old,
paints like a five-year-old.

Painting by Pam, 5¾ years

the child at five years

Collage by Daphne, 5½ years

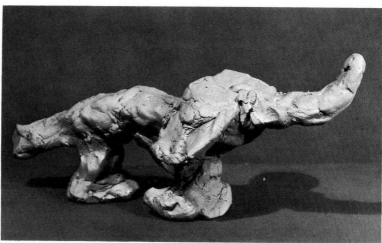

Elephant by Mitchell, 5¾ years

Construction by Fredi, 5 years

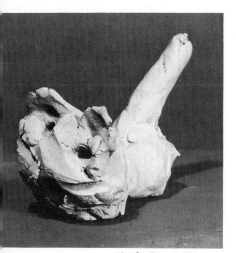

Cat by Loren, 5¼ years

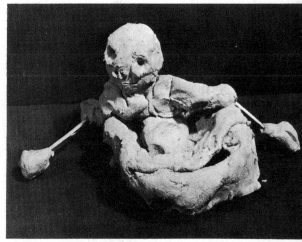

Man Rowing a Boat by Tony, 5 years

31

the child at five years

Mobile by Carol, 5½ years

Lady by Joan, 5½ years

growth in the painting of two three-year-olds over a short period

While there is a general development in the young child's growth from three to five years, there is also evidence of growth over short periods of time. Because children are unique, the characteristics of their expression are different. This series of paintings illustrates both the uniqueness and development of two three-year-olds over a period of approximately seven weeks. The class met for one hour each week.

The first child, Elizabeth (pages 34–35), started out making free, separate masses of color, mixing colors on her paper. She continued to do this for several weeks, each time mixing new colors and bringing the shapes closer together. Then she began uniting the shapes with linear forms, and the last painting is enriched with staccato brush strokes.

In Michael's paintings (pages 36–37) we can see that he paints in a more linear fashion than does Elizabeth. In his first painting he merely made vertical strokes with his brush. After a few weeks he started combining vertical and curved lines. He has formed shapes with his lines in the last painting, and has reinforced this discovery by strengthening one of them with masses of color.

The three paintings representing each child's growth are selected from a number more than twice as large made over the seven-week period. The motifs used are ones that the children happened to invent or choose at the particular time. This in no way implies that all three-year-olds use these or that Elizabeth and Michael will continue using them over a long period of time. The method of exploring and the inventiveness employed are the important factors.

1

2

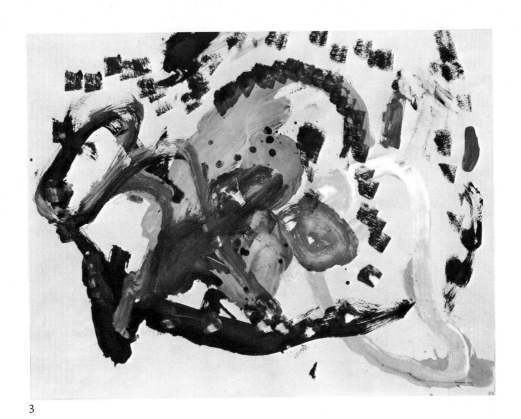

3

Paintings by Elizabeth, 3 years

2

3

Paintings by Michael, 3 years

growth in children's paintings over an extended period

There is no precise pattern of development for each age level. Not all three-year-olds behave alike, nor are they completely different from four-year-olds. There is an evident and gradual growth process that almost every child goes through, from the first tentative exploration to greater sureness in the control of material and expression. Although the following development is illustrated through painting, the same is true in modeling, collage, or construction.

When a young child uses poster paint for the first time, he will dip his brush into a color and make tentative strokes on the paper. It is a pleasure to watch his face light up with delight as he discovers what he can do with his brush. The colors in his first paintings are clear, unmixed, and usually separated from each other.

He soon discovers, however that by painting one color over another while the first is still wet, he can make a new color, and he will concentrate on changing colors in this way. As he does this, the colors become muddy. These paintings look quite different from his first ones. They are less attractive but they represent a forward step in his development.

Later, he will mix colors less haphazardly and will begin to paint them next to each other rather than on top of each other. Some children tend to cover the whole paper with paint, whereas others will leave part of the paper unpainted.

As he gains control over his materials, a child will gradually begin making different linear shapes with his brush. Often he paints a solid color within these shapes and sometimes decorates them with other colors.

Frequently the shapes he has painted will remind a child of something he knows and he will turn them into apartment buildings, or people, or other subjects.

1. Painting by Pete, 3 years

2. Painting by Amy, 3 years

3. Painting by Betty, 3 years

4. Painting by Debbie, 4 years

5. Painting by Susan, 4 years

41

the child's first art experience

Usually adults think of art in terms of painting pictures or making sculpture. Actually, when a child makes new and interesting combinations while building with blocks, or when he arranges and rearranges such things as shells, acorns, or pebbles into designs, he is developing his creative power. He is discovering that he can express his ideas and feelings with the materials at hand.

Parents are the child's first art teachers because the child has his earliest art experiences at home. Not only the casual things surrounding him but particularly his toys, books, and playthings have tremendous influence upon the young child's developing taste and should be chosen with an eye toward their potentialities for creative play.

The child's initial experience with art materials, such as paint or clay, should come when he can handle them constructively. This doesn't mean, of course, that his approach will be the same as that of most adults. For instance, he may enjoy just putting paint on the paper or mixing colors together to make new ones, or squeezing the clay between his fingers. It is important to remember that this is a new adventure for him and that these seemingly random motions are exciting discoveries.

If he can manipulate brush and paint, he is ready for the experience. Most children are ready and eager for this at three. Some two-year-olds can handle materials adequately and get great satisfaction from doing so. Although other children may not be ready until they are four, their satisfaction and pleasure in the experience will be just as great as though they had started earlier.

If a child pours paint on the table or floor or persistently dabbles in the water, put the paints away and try them another time, when he is ready to use them with more purpose. This holds true of other materials as well. If a child pats and squeezes clay, enjoying what he can do with it, give him the opportunity to experiment, but if he throws it around, or eats it, then wait until he is ready to approach it more constructively. Many three-year-olds can cut with scissors and handle paste adequately, on their own level. However, if a child is not able to manipulate scissors until he is four, or five, then that is the time for him to start. Some three-year-olds pour paste over the table and themselves. If they persist in this, it would be wise to wait a while and offer it later.

Each child should have his first art experience when he is ready for it. Naturally, this will not be the same for all children because no two children are alike, nor do they grow at the same rate.

2

fundamentals of art education

Adults often ask, "When should fundamentals be taught?" One should ask them in turn, "What do you mean by fundamentals? Do you mean only skills such as accuracy and representation or d you mean helping a child to find his own way to put on paper or to shape in clay what he is seeing and feeling?"

Many adults remember the kind of drawing lessons they struggled with as children —drawing the shape of a box or the ellipse of a vase, or trying to make a house that looked exactly like the one the teacher had in mind. If such objectives are thought of as fundamentals, should one not ask himself what he actually learned from these lessons and whether they helped to make him able and eager to continue with drawing and painting? At the Art Center it is recognized that there are fundamentals which are much more basic than such isolated and limited skills.

Giving a child opportunity and time to explore and encouraging him to do so is fundamental to his growth in art. What he paints, models, or constructs may not be recognizable to others or appear "finished" according to adult standards. As a matter of fact, the child probably has not been working toward a "finished" result at all but has concentrated on changing what he has been making and enjoyed the satisfaction in his power to do so. He has finished when he has had a complete experience and is ready to go on to something else. It may seem that what the child has started has been completely obliterated because he has painted one thing upon another without bothering to take a new sheet of paper or has covered up his collage by pasting a piece of paper over it. From his viewpoint, he hasn't obliterated anything. He knows that what he has made is still there and he is confident in this knowledge. It is the process of doing rather than the final product that is important to the child.

It is fundamental to provide young children with the opportunity and encouragement to express freely their ideas and feelings. Through such media as fluid paint and soft clay, creative activity can be a vivid language through which a young child can tell about his experiences. Everyone needs some outlet for his feelings. Sometimes these may be so vague and diffused that the child has not been able to put them into words. The fact is becoming recognized that the more ways we have to express our feelings, the happier and healthier we are apt to be.

Acceptance and respect for what the child creates is fundamental. Children are eager to please their parents, teachers, and other adults close to them. When a child feels that what he has been making is not respected, he is likely to try to do something

44

that he thinks will be acceptable. If this happens, he probably will never again feel quite as free or confident in his own expression. This was true of Eleanor who is nearly six years old. When she was just five, she had happily made many paintings in a class at the Art Center. The following year she returned to the class and announced that she had been to a birthday party and would make a picture of it. She started to draw but before long began to show signs of dissatisfaction and discomfort. When her teacher asked whether she might help, Eleanor said unhappily that her drawing wasn't right. The teacher said that it certainly looked all right to her, but Eleanor insisted that the table wasn't right and her teacher soon realized that some well-meaning person had been trying to teach Eleanor to draw in perspective. Despite efforts to clarify her ideas and reassure her, she became more and more confused and finally turned her paper over and aimlessly smeared paint on it. Then she said, "I have a headache and can't paint any more." All her pleasure and satisfaction in painting had been wiped out by an adult who had the best intentions but lacked understanding and respect for a child's expression in art. It will take a long time to re-establish Eleanor's confidence in her ability to express herself in her own way.

Young children paint or model what they know or feel. They are not particularly concerned with reproducing what they see. Perspective has no meaning for them, for example, converging lines of receding tracks are only a triangular shape to a child who draws railroad tracks the way they actually are, in parallel lines.

It is fundamental to learn techniques as they are needed. A child can learn what he needs to know about a brush when he is painting. He can be shown how to wash his brush before dipping it from one color into another and how to press it on a sponge or rag in order to wipe out excess dirty water. Gradually he will learn to keep his colors clean. If he holds his brush so that it wobbles the teacher or parent can suggest that another way may be easier for him. He can learn how to mix colors and make new ones. He can learn to fasten things. For instance, if he wants to stick two pieces of clay together he can be shown that if he rubs his finger where he joined them so that no crack shows the pieces will stay together. When the child has had a lot of experience squeezing and patting clay he can be encouraged to do other things with it such as rolling it into coils. Many different things can be made from coils. When a child is baffled because he is not putting paste on a piece of paper so that it will stick to another piece, one can show him where to put the paste.

There is neither enjoyment nor creative growth in this type of indoctrinary learning.

Techniques have no value in themselves. If taught before they are needed, they have no meaning for a child and only confuse him. A child learns to paint, model, and construct as he learns to walk—slowly, developing in his own way and learning each new step in the process as he is ready for it.

Parents sometimes say, "My child does much better at home than in a class." Recently, when a mother said this, the teacher asked, "Does he draw with pencil or crayon at home, or are you talking about painting? Do you mean that he draws objects which are recognizable to you?" The mother admitted that she was thinking about crayon drawings which she could recognize.

Young children are apt to make more recognizable forms with pencil and crayon than with paint, and when it is easier for adults to understand the content of drawings they tend to prefer them to the less intelligible paintings. Perhaps also the fact that drawings appear neater makes them more attractive to some adults. However, the parent who understands what painting can mean to young children sees in their paintings values which are not at first apparent. The two media and their functions, therefore, should not be confused. Adults who appreciate what children do will not prefer one medium over another and will be able to reinforce children's security in their own ability.

The crayon drawing above was made at home by Leslie, 4½ years;
she made the painting below at school. Leslie brought the crayon
drawing she had made at home as a gift to her teacher the same day
that she made the painting.

3

how adults can help

fostering independence

That child is lucky indeed whose parents and teachers are as delighted with each forward step in the language of art as they are with each new venture in speech. Adults will help the child best if they understand what he is trying to do. Understanding underlies respect and this goes deeper than mere cordial acceptance. The child needs respect in order to go forward with confidence in what he has to say and in his mastery of the means to say it. How can adults gain this understanding? For one thing they can watch a child as he works. His expression of absorption, of attentiveness, of pleasure, is as telling as the spoken word or the finished product.

Another way to encourage children is to share their experiences. Parents can work along with their children although they should not show them what to make, or how to make it, or give them things to copy. Naturally the way parents and children work will be quite different. Parents should expect these differences and be pleased that the child is working independently. They can start sharing by helping the child get out his materials. A parent might say: "I'll get the paints and you get out the paper," or "Why don't you get out the clay and I'll put newspaper around the table and floor." Giving the child this responsibility will help him to become independent in caring for his own art materials. Perhaps when mother is shopping, she can find something for the collage treasure box and say, "Look what I've found, do you think we could use this in a paste picture?" All of this heightens the feeling of "togetherness." The parents' interest fosters the child's feeling that what he is doing has value.

It is, of course, not possible or even necessary for a busy parent to be with a child every minute that he is painting or constructing. If the child feels an adult's sincere interest in what he is making, he will gain confidence to go ahead. Parents should try to look at what a child shows them with an understanding eye. He may have been experimenting with paints or other materials in order to gain power over them. Adults should never feel that time spent in experimentation is wasted because no finished product comes out of it. A quicker result might be obtained by having the child follow rules, but it will have little or no meaning for him.

Experimenting is not just finding out what paint, clay, or other materials can do. A child also experiments with expressing in concrete form his ideas and feelings about what is happening to him in his own world. Thus he strengthens his power to weigh choices, to decide, and to face the results of his decisions. Painting or modeling may be pleasurable but it is also serious business.

48

Sometimes it may seem as though materials have hardly been set up before the child announces that he is finished. Parents and teachers should not be troubled by this. The child may have had just as satisfying an experience as one who has worked for a longer time. The quality of an experience should not be measured in terms of duration of time. Sometimes a child may not want to paint at a particular time. This does not necessarily mean that he doesn't like painting. He may be absorbed in another activity, or it is possible that his confidence has been shaken because he has been made to feel inadequate by someone whom he is anxious to please.

If a child asks for help, he may not be needing the specific thing he asks for. Perhaps at that particular time he wants only to be assured of interest. A three-year-old seldom asks for help. Four- and five-year-olds whose work has been respected on their own level will also go ahead independently. Unless a child shows genuine dissatisfaction with what he has made, adults should accept it without offering criticism. However, if Johnny asks: "Show me how to make a horse," or anything else, no matter how flattering this may be to his mother and father, or how much they like to do things for their child, they should realize that he is harmed instead of helped when they show him how to do it their way rather than encouraging him to do it his way. They might help him clarify his own idea by comments such as: "What kind of a horse do you want to make? What color? What is he doing? If I show you my way, it will be my horse, not yours."

Sometimes, for one reason or another, a child may feel that he must conform to adult standards and he may ask, "What shall I paint?" If he does, an adult should not feel obligated to tell him to paint a tree with apples, or a house, or a boat, or anything else. He might say some such thing as: "There are so many things you can think of that I can't," or "Did you see any pretty colors today? How about trying to paint as many different colors as possible on your paper," or "Why not make what you like best to play with," or "Let's try to see how many different things the brush can do." Often a new medium, such as clay or collage, will encourage a child to explore and work in his own way.

Such suggestions may help him to get started but if a child persistently asks for help and ideas, he may have become too dependent on others. The real problem is to reinstate his self-confidence. Perhaps giving him more responsibility in doing things for himself and for others, such as washing his own hands, dressing himself, caring for pets, getting things for mother, might help. Trust and confidence in his ability to carry out responsibilities on his own level can help him to feel that his contribution is of real worth.

Sharing what they know about a child can help parents and teachers understand his problems and work together toward helping him grow. If a child is going to school, parents should make every effort to become acquainted with the school program. This can help them to strike a balance between what happens there and what the child does at home. If the school program is sound, parents can learn many things from the teacher that they can adapt to the home situation. On the other hand, no matter how much experience a teacher may have had with large numbers of children, talking with a parent can give her an insight into the particular needs of an individual child. Parents can also help a teacher who is struggling to better her program in the light of new ideas in art education. A group of parents supporting a teacher can often make it possible for an administrator to change a difficult situation.

Sometimes parents are faced with the problem of their children attending a school still using outmoded methods in art education, such as copying or tracing patterns. They should not undermine the child's respect for his teacher or school, but if the child seems disturbed, one thing they can say is: "At school why don't you do it their way, but at home let's do it your own way. It's more fun."

However, if the art program at school is so outmoded or if the school has no art program at all, parents should try to do something to remedy this. Parent-teacher organizations have been created for just such purposes. Some parents may feel that it is not up to them to be concerned with the school program, although actually it is their responsibility since, after all, schools exist for the children who attend them. Parent-teacher organizations, rather than hindering, can reinforce the hands of teachers and administrators in building better programs for children.

Children do the kind of work above under the guidance of teachers who respect and understand their creative growth. The work below is the result of indoctrinary teaching, which is still carried on in schools where the art program is outmoded.

providing materials and a place to work

Parents can play an important part in stimulating the child's interest and growth by setting up a place for him to work and by providing the proper materials.

A child needs an inviting place even if it is only a free corner in the kitchen or living room. It is important that materials should be available so that they can be gotten out readily when they are to be used. If a child is eager to paint, waiting for elaborate preparations may dampen his enthusiasm for the entire activity. Children and parents can set up a working place together. As a child becomes familiar with the best way of getting out what he needs, he will be able to start by himself even when his mother is busy. Of course, she will want to keep an eye on his progress so that she can help him if necessary and be ready to supervise cleaning up when his creative energy is spent.

Equipment need not be elaborate. A low table, with a surface large enough to hold good-sized paper and a tray of paints, is excellent for painting and will also serve for working in clay, collage, or construction. The table should be low enough for the child to see and reach the whole of his paper. If the top is slippery, a bit of masking tape stuck across an edge of the paper onto the table will keep the paper from sliding. Oilcloth or newspaper can be spread on both the table and the floor to protect surfaces and make cleaning up easier. A smock or one of father's old shirts with sleeves cut short will protect the child's clothes. A set of low shelves should be nearby to hold a variety of materials and tools such as paper, brushes, and collage and construction materials. If shelves are at least eighteen inches deep, eighteen- by twenty-four-inch drawing paper can be stored on one of them. If not, a portfolio of the same size or a little larger will serve the purpose. This may be kept behind the shelves or in a closet. If there is no space for a set of shelves, the materials and tools may be kept together in a box or carton or in a drawer which can be pulled out and carried about from place to place.

An easel is also desirable for painting. One advantage of the easel is that the child's paper is up where he can easily see and reach his painting as he works. However, the disadvantage is that the child has much less control over the paint, which tends to flow together and run down the paper. Many children, therefore, prefer to work on a table or the floor. When working on the floor, spread out newspapers and put the paper to be worked on, the tray of paints, and water dish on it. Set them against a wall or in a corner, so that they will not be kicked over or stepped on. If an easel is preferred, and a commercially made one seems too expensive, a good substitute is a piece of beaverboard set against the wall or on the seat of a straight chair leaning against the back.

Clay should be stored in an airtight container such as a crock or large can to keep it moist. Wrapping the container with a plastic material will help keep out air. If this is placed in a wooden box or on a platform set on casters, it can be wheeled out of the way under a table when not in use.

The child will need a box to hold his collection of things such as shells, feathers, yarn, wire, and cloth for making collages. A box or tray with divisions, like a refrigerator tray or jewelry box, is very useful for holding the very small things like buttons and beads; the larger things can be put in a pasteboard box.

The materials out of which the child creates are important to his satisfaction and success. Often a parent goes to the expense of buying materials which are a hindrance to the young child or are too elaborate or advanced, such as a complicated set of crayons of forty-eight colors or oil paints. The following are recommended as most suitable for creative growth at this age level.

Poster paint. Poster paint is the best kind of paint for children because it flows easily from the brush onto the paper. It comes in brilliant colors and, since it is opaque, a child can change colors by painting one over the other. Blue, red, yellow, black, and white are adequate, because almost any color can be obtained by mixing two or more of these. Green, orange, and violet may be added if a wider range is desired. It is economical to buy poster paint in pint, or even quart, jars. Paints must always be kept covered, to prevent them from drying out. Glass syrup dispensers with metal tops make good containers for storing paint. If the tops are kept clean, the colors can be poured without spilling.

Powder paint. Powder paint costs less than poster paint and is almost as good when mixed with water to the consistency of heavy cream. It is less convenient, however, as it sours quickly and must be mixed each time in small quantities. Watercolors that usually come in hard little cakes lack the freeing qualities of poster paint and are not desirable for young children.

Tools for painting. For the child's use, small containers, one for each color, such as glass or plastic furniture coasters, or small jar tops, should be provided. Brushes, a large container for water (a plastic bowl or a coffee can will do), and an acetate sponge for wiping the brushes are also needed. It is desirable to place all of these on a tray (an aluminum cookie sheet makes a good tray). Three brushes, three-quarter-, one-half-, and one-quarter-inch, are all that the young child needs. Flat, long-handled, short bristle brushes called "brights" are the best. The child should use large brushes, three-quarter- or one-half-inch, for most work and the narrow one-quarter-inch brush only for details. Children often paint with the sponge as well as with the brush. Brushes should be thoroughly washed after the painting period so that all paint is out of them and stored either bristle end up or lying flat in order to keep bristles in shape.

Chalk. Large soft chalk comes in many colors and can be used when, for one reason or another, it is too difficult to set up poster paints, or to introduce another medium. By using the broad side of the chalk, the child will get quite rich color. New colors can be mixed by rubbing one color over another. The best kind of chalk is lecturer's chalk, which is approximately half an inch square.

Equipment for working at home

Materials for collage

Crayons. Crayons should not be confused with chalks; and one certainly should never accept them as a substitute for poster paint. Crayons are less expensive and less messy but they do not stimulate a child toward exploration and experimentation as poster paint does. Also a child is apt to grip the crayon more tightly and become tense as his interest increases rather than to relax as in painting. Crayons and pencils lend themselves to a linear form of expression and as such are media in which children tend to make narrative or story-telling pictures. Young children also make zig-zag lines with pencil or crayon in imitation of adult writing. It would be a mistake to insist that they fill in forms with color when using crayon.

Paper. There are many kinds of paper suitable for painting. White drawing paper is the most expensive and the best. A light-weight manila paper is less expensive but not so durable and since it is yellowish it is often not so inviting to work on. Unprinted newsprint is usable but it is flimsy. Any one of these will do but all can be used at different times. Paper can be bought in pads or by the ream (a package of 500 sheets). It is also sold in rolls and, although easier to store in this form, it has the disadvantage of having to be cut each time. Paper should be large, approximately eighteen by twenty-four inches in size. Wrapping paper or newspaper, especially those pages with a uniform small type printing, such as the financial or want-ad sections, are good substitutes when other paper is not available. It is better for a child to have plenty of paper on which to experiment than to be limited to a few sheets no matter how good they may be.

Clay. Clay can be squeezed and pounded but at the same time is firm enough to hold its shape. A child can make and remake things with it. It can serve as a base for constructions using such things as tongue depressors, swab sticks, popsicle sticks, twigs, and acorns. The best to buy is moist clay, a powdered clay mixed with water which hardens when it dries. This should not be confused with plasticine, which is often sold in colored strips or cubes. Plasticine is clay mixed with oil. It does not harden, is rubbery and less pleasant to touch than moist clay. Moist clay can be bought in various quantities, such as five-, ten-, and twenty-five-pound tins, or hundred-pound drums. It is better to buy it in larger quantities if it can be kept moist. It should be put into a crock with a tight cover or plastic bag with a zipper, or wrapped in plastic, since it must be kept airtight to stay moist. The clay comes in a large mass or lump. If it is difficult to get out in small pieces one may cut into it with the end of a heavy wire clothes hanger using a scooping motion and then lift the cut pieces out.

Finger paint. Finger paint, like clay, can be easily manipulated. However, even though finger painting is often a freeing experience, it is not a demanding one, and therefore offers little opportunity for growth. It is quite different from painting with a brush, in which developing control leads to increasing ability to express feelings and ideas. Finger paint can satisfy the child who has the need to be messy. If a child insists on putting his hands into poster paint, perhaps he needs to finger paint for a while. It is not necessary to do finger painting on paper. A table with a plastic top or the common enamel-top kitchen table makes a good surface, where the whole thing can be wiped up easily afterward. A piece of oil cloth firmly fastened on any table provides a good surface on which to finger paint.

Construction paper and scissors. Paper and scissors respond to the child's need to change and invent because he can produce new shapes with them. Paper can be cut or torn into many different shapes, or rolled, folded, and changed in a variety of ways. Scissors should be blunt-ended but of good quality so that they have sharp blades. Paper for cutting must be firm, such as construction paper, heavy wrapping paper, corrugated or any strong paper. Flimsy paper, like tissue, doesn't offer enough resistance.

Collage materials. A collage is a two-dimensional design made out of different materials fastened together. The materials out of which a child makes collages include an almost infinite variety of things, manufactured or found in nature. These may range from fabrics, paper, metal, and plastic to leaves, bark, and shells.

As was mentioned earlier, the collage experience helps develop a child's tactile powers and gives him an opportunity to make selections and judgments which are basic to his growth and taste. The opportunity for choice should, therefore, be wide and include variety in color—bright or neutral; in texture—soft, hard, smooth, rough; in pattern—geometric or natural forms, large or small motifs. Many things which often go into the wastebasket can be useful, such as cellophane from cigarette packages, ribbon or gay wrappings from birthday or Christmas gifts. In addition, it is advisable to purchase something special now and then, like fluorescent, colored, or metallic paper, or perhaps some tinseled string from the five and dime or department store. These will not only give variety to the child's collection, but will be added encouragement for him to realize that his parents are interested in his creative efforts and, therefore, in him.

Some children make collages by sticking materials together, one on another. Most children, however, need a firm piece of paper or cardboard on which to arrange and fasten the materials they have selected. For example, construction paper or the cardboard put into shirts by the laundry can be used for bases. For sticking things together, library paste which comes in a jar with a brush is preferred by young children, but mucilage in small bottles with dispenser tops can also be used if it is more convenient.

Construction materials. Three-dimensional constructions are called mobiles and stabiles. Mobiles are designs made with a variety of materials fastened to a wire structure or hanging on strings, or attached in some other way, to produce motion. Motion is the principal characteristic of a mobile. A stabile is a combination of forms made of different materials but which has no motion, as its name implies.

Both mobiles and stabiles are made of practically every kind of material and their construction and composition can be very complex or elaborate. The simplest and most spontaneous methods are recommended for the young child, to conform to his abilities and skill. The same materials recommended above for collage are suitable for constructions, with the addition of such things as wire of different gauges but light enough so the child can bend them easily. Millinery wire, copper or brass wire of gauges sixteen, twenty, and twenty-three, are good. Bell wire which comes in different colors and wire solder are also suitable and can be purchased in the local hardware store. Long pipe cleaners are excellent and can be found in florist shops. A base is necessary for starting. A lump of clay makes the simplest base in which a child, particularly a three-year-old, can stick such things as straws, shells, swab sticks, or whatever he chooses. Another is to staple the pipe cleaner to a cardboard square. Styrofoam, a plastic that looks like snow, comes in blocks about an inch thick; it can be cut into any size and shape and because of its soft but sturdy texture a child can push pipe cleaners or small sticks into it. A single pipe cleaner, wire, or cardboard with holes punched in it hanging from a string is good for starting mobiles. While mobiles are often made on a string or wire, they can also be made like stabiles; that is, wires, pipe cleaners, or straws can be fastened to a base and shapes of various materials fastened to their upper ends with string or fine wire, so that they move.

Child working at improvised easel at home

PRINTED IN DENMARK BY EGMONT H. PETERSEN, COPENHAGEN